RISE&GRIND

MORNING SUCCESS JOURNAL

The Tool To Achieving Your Goals In 100 Days Or Less

CREATED BY JEREMY WARLEN

Name: _____

Date: _____

Cover Photos By-

Daniel Yates

Instagram / @Unsighted

Youtube / Unsighted

ISBN-13:
978-1544184944

ISBN-10:
1544184948

RISE & GRIND

Morning Success Journal

Hello, my name is Jeremy Warlen. I am a serial entrepreneur. I am very ambitious and focused on the things that I want out of life. Not too long ago, I started an Instagram Motivation Page- @RetireBeforeYourParents; and I would get emails from my followers asking, "How can you do all these different things and still be making actual progress?" Or better yet, "How can someone even more successful and a busier than I am, achieve their goals?"

That's a great question, because most of us have tons of ideas and goals in our head, but since we feel like we have so many, we get overwhelmed and end up not doing a single thing. So the answer to that question is, in a world full of distractions you need to have a laser like **FOCUS** on the goals you want to accomplish. That's how successful people do it.

Its been proven, that writing down your goals imprints in your mind as a task to get done. The problem is most people only write down their goals once a year on New Year's Eve and never create a plan or a deadline or nothing to achieve this goal. They just write it down and wish for it. Well, successful people do things differently. They have trained their mind to be seriously focused on whatever they desire. This book is a great tool to get you focused on your next big life target. It will help you get a clear view and figure out the steps you will need to take.

Repetition is the way to seriously train your brain on figuring out what you need to reach your main goal. The Rise & Grind Morning Success Journal is a very simple method that only takes 5-10 minutes each morning. So let's face it, if you don't have 5 minutes to get a plan ready for your goal, your goal won't ever be achieved.

How The Journal Pages Works

10 Day Plan of Attack- We break down the 100 days into 10 day increments. So you will have to do a Plan of Attack ten different times throughout this journal. This makes the goals be more manageable. This page will help you figure out your major steps and schedule what your next ten days look like. Do these pages the day or the night before you start your next ten days.

Daily Routine- Each morning before you check your phone or turn on the news, take 5 minutes to figure out how you are going to get one step closer to your major life goal. Get your mind clear and focused on the target. Then go execute the steps you have planned.

Clear Your Mind- Every day you will need to get rid of the clutter in your mind that may distract you from getting your goals done. The best way to get rid of that clutter is writing it all out. Get all your negative emotions out on this page because you have more important stuff to take up your time.

10 Day Review- Just like the *10 Day Plan of Attack,* you will end up doing the *10 Day Review* ten different times as well. This is where you have to be honest with yourself and give yourself a score on how you felt you did these past ten days. Throughout the ten days, you have found out what works and what doesn't, the review will help you focus on what you need to do more of.

Set SMART Goals for Yourself

S is for **Specific**. Specific goals have a much better chance at being achieved. To set a specific goal you must know- Who, What, When, Where, Why, How.

M is for **Measurable**. You need to make your goals measurable. Include dates, deadlines, amounts etc. in your goals. Here is an example; let's say your goal is simply "to lose weight," well how will you know when you have been successful? In 10 days you lose 1 pound or in 100 days and you lose 30 pounds? Without a way to measure your goal, you will miss out on the celebration of achieving your goal.

A is for **Attainable.** Make sure the goals you set are possible to achieve. Yet, don't make them too easy for yourself either. You need to set realistic yet challenging goals to see the best results.

R is for **Relevant.** Your goals should be relevant to the direction you want your life and career to take. By keeping your goals aligned with this, you will develop the focus you need to get anything you want.

T is for **Time-Bound.** Having a deadline creates a sense of urgency and makes you get things done faster.

Follow

One

Course

Until

Success

1st 10 Day Plan of Attack

What is your main goal you want to achieve in 100 days?

I WILL HAVE A NEW JOB BY SEPTEMBER 21st

Name three major steps you would like to achieve these next 10 days.

prepare resume and cover letter

record and upload question videos

apply at smartcity atx

Schedule your major steps for the next Ten Days.

Day One: ~~gather references~~ ✓

Day Two: ~~update cover letter~~ ✓

Day Three: upload (experience summary)

Day Four: ~~rough draft questions~~

Day Five: (upload written questions)

Day Six: ~~prepare to record video questions~~

Day Seven (record video questions)

Day Eight: upload resume to linkedin ✱

Day Nine: finalize

Day Ten: submit application

Day 1

What is today's main goal? Make sure this step will get you closer to your 100 day goal.

finalize a list of references w/ information

Why do you want to achieve this goal? Be specific. Give this goal a meaning.

- it is essential for any and every application
- there are wonderful people in my life who want to see me succeed and will support me in my success, but i must do the work the give them that opportunity

Write three ways you can accomplish today's main goal.

1.) select 5 supporters
2.) reach out to each
3.) type that shit up

Clear You're Mind

This is Important.

Get anything out of your head that may be a distraction from today's goal on this page.

dario reeves - ~~hospitality manager~~ special projects trainer

holly hoffman - real estate agent

taylor higdon - special projects manager

chilo mendoza - director of opporations

Jennifer zulliani - hospitality manager

brittnee anaya - GSM

- phone #
- email
- title
- location

Day 2

What is today's main goal? Make sure this step will get you closer to your 100 day goal.

update cover letter

Why do you want to achieve this goal? Be specific. Give this goal a meaning.

Show em' your goodies
(at least a preview)

Write three ways you can accomplish today's main goal.

just do it
just do it
just do it

Clear You're Mind

This is Important.

Get anything out of your head that may be a distraction from today's goal on this page.

Day 3

What is today's main goal? Make sure this step will get you closer to your 100 day goal.

draft experience summary

Why do you want to achieve this goal? Be specific. Give this goal a meaning.

_____

_____

_____

_____

_____

_____

Write three ways you can accomplish today's main goal.

_____

_____

_____

_____

_____

_____

Clear You're Mind

This is Important.

Get anything out of your head that may be a distraction from today's goal on this page.

AVEDA SPA AND SALON   * cash tips
                                only
11:00am dual exfoliation peel $55
— manicure $15 (+plant peel?)
— cut and condition

AVENUE MASSAGE
—, 80 min $35
— mud + 30 min $60
— scalp +oil massage $ 15

Day 4

What is today's main goal? Make sure this step will get you closer to your 100 day goal.

every detail finalized : questions , summary , linkedin

Why do you want to achieve this goal? Be specific. Give this goal a meaning.

to be able to SUMIT APPLICATION !!
you're so close sister you got this.
30 minutes of laser focused energy

Write three ways you can accomplish today's main goal.

*meditate with questions
* avoid distractions
* 30 minute introvals

Clear You're Mind

This is Important.

Get anything out of your head that may be a distraction from today's goal on this page.

- 10:30 oil
- 11:00 - facial
  1:30
- 1:30 - write questions by pool ?
  LUNCH
- gym

Day 5

What is today's main goal? Make sure this step will get you closer to your 100 day goal.

_____

Why do you want to achieve this goal? Be specific. Give this goal a meaning.

_____

_____

_____

_____

_____

Write three ways you can accomplish today's main goal.

_____

_____

_____

_____

_____

Clear You're Mind

This is Important.

Get anything out of your head that may be a distraction from today's goal on this page.

you got this.

Day 6

What is today's main goal? Make sure this step will get you closer to your 100 day goal.

_____

Why do you want to achieve this goal? Be specific. Give this goal a meaning.

_____

_____

_____

_____

_____

Write three ways you can accomplish today's main goal.

_____

_____

_____

_____

_____

_____

Clear You're Mind

This is Important.

Get anything out of your head that may be a distraction from today's goal on this page.

Day 7

What is today's main goal? Make sure this step will get you closer to your 100 day goal.

_____

Why do you want to achieve this goal? Be specific. Give this goal a meaning.

_____

_____

_____

_____

_____

Write three ways you can accomplish today's main goal.

_____

_____

_____

_____

_____

Clear You're Mind

This is Important.

Get anything out of your head that may be a distraction from today's goal on this page.

Day 8

What is today's main goal? Make sure this step will get you closer to your 100 day goal.

_____

Why do you want to achieve this goal? Be specific. Give this goal a meaning.

_____

_____

_____

_____

_____

Write three ways you can accomplish today's main goal.

_____

_____

_____

_____

_____

_____

Clear You're Mind

This is Important.

Get anything out of your head that may be a distraction from today's goal on this page.

Day 9

What is today's main goal? Make sure this step will get you closer to your 100 day goal.

_____

Why do you want to achieve this goal? Be specific. Give this goal a meaning.

_____

_____

_____

_____

_____

_____

Write three ways you can accomplish today's main goal.

_____

_____

_____

_____

_____

_____

Clear You're Mind

This is Important.

Get anything out of your head that may be a distraction from today's goal on this page.

Day 10

What is today's main goal? Make sure this step will get you closer to your 100 day goal.

_____

Why do you want to achieve this goal? Be specific. Give this goal a meaning.

_____

_____

_____

_____

_____

Write three ways you can accomplish today's main goal.

_____

_____

_____

_____

_____

Clear You're Mind

This is Important.

Get anything out of your head that may be a distraction from today's goal on this page.

10 Day Review

Rate how you feel you did these past 10 days.

1 being poor, 10 being excellent

1 2 3 4 5 6 7 8 9 10

How close are you to your 100 day goal?

_____

_____

_____

Name the things you wish you could have accomplished, but did not these past 10 days.

_____

_____

_____

_____

2nd 10 Day Plan of Attack

What is your main goal you want to achieve in 100 days?

_____

Name three major steps you would like to achieve these next 10 days.

_____

_____

_____

Schedule your major steps for the next Ten Days.

Day One: _____

Day Two: _____

Day Three: _____

Day Four: _____

Day Five: _____

Day Six: _____

Day Seven: _____

Day Eight: _____

Day Nine: _____

Day Ten: _____

Day 11

What is today's main goal? Make sure this step will get you closer to your 100 day goal.

_____

Why do you want to achieve this goal? Be specific. Give this goal a meaning.

_____

_____

_____

_____

_____

_____

Write three ways you can accomplish today's main goal.

_____

_____

_____

_____

_____

_____

Clear You're Mind

This is Important.

Get anything out of your head that may be a distraction from today's goal on this page.

Day 12

What is today's main goal? Make sure this step will get you closer to your 100 day goal.

_____

Why do you want to achieve this goal? Be specific. Give this goal a meaning.

_____

_____

_____

_____

_____

_____

Write three ways you can accomplish today's main goal.

_____

_____

_____

_____

_____

_____

Clear You're Mind

This is Important.

Get anything out of your head that may be a distraction from today's goal on this page.

REMINDER- THIS JOURNAL DOESN'T WORK IF YOU DON'T.

Day 13

What is today's main goal? Make sure this step will get you closer to your 100 day goal.

_____

Why do you want to achieve this goal? Be specific. Give this goal a meaning.

_____

_____

_____

_____

_____

Write three ways you can accomplish today's main goal.

_____

_____

_____

_____

_____

Clear You're Mind

This is Important.

Get anything out of your head that may be a distraction from today's goal on this page.

Day 14

What is today's main goal? Make sure this step will get you closer to your 100 day goal.

_____

Why do you want to achieve this goal? Be specific. Give this goal a meaning.

_____

_____

_____

_____

_____

_____

Write three ways you can accomplish today's main goal.

_____

_____

_____

_____

_____

_____

Clear You're Mind

This is Important.

Get anything out of your head that may be a distraction from today's goal on this page.

REMINDER- THIS JOURNAL DOESN'T WORK IF YOU DON'T.

Day 15

What is today's main goal? Make sure this step will get you closer to your 100 day goal.

_____

Why do you want to achieve this goal? Be specific. Give this goal a meaning.

_____

_____

_____

_____

_____

_____

Write three ways you can accomplish today's main goal.

_____

_____

_____

_____

_____

_____

Clear You're Mind

This is Important.

Get anything out of your head that may be a distraction from today's goal on this page.

Day 16

What is today's main goal? Make sure this step will get you closer to your 100 day goal.

_____

Why do you want to achieve this goal? Be specific. Give this goal a meaning.

_____

_____

_____

_____

_____

_____

Write three ways you can accomplish today's main goal.

_____

_____

_____

_____

_____

_____

Clear You're Mind

This is Important.

Get anything out of your head that may be a distraction from today's goal on this page.

Day 17

What is today's main goal? Make sure this step will get you closer to your 100 day goal.

_____

Why do you want to achieve this goal? Be specific. Give this goal a meaning.

_____

_____

_____

_____

_____

Write three ways you can accomplish today's main goal.

_____

_____

_____

_____

_____

Clear You're Mind

This is Important.

Get anything out of your head that may be a distraction from today's goal on this page.

Day 18

What is today's main goal? Make sure this step will get you closer to your 100 day goal.

_____

Why do you want to achieve this goal? Be specific. Give this goal a meaning.

_____

_____

_____

_____

_____

Write three ways you can accomplish today's main goal.

_____

_____

_____

_____

_____

_____

Clear You're Mind

This is Important.

Get anything out of your head that may be a distraction from today's goal on this page.

Day 19

What is today's main goal? Make sure this step will get you closer to your 100 day goal.

_____

Why do you want to achieve this goal? Be specific. Give this goal a meaning.

_____

_____

_____

_____

_____

_____

Write three ways you can accomplish today's main goal.

_____

_____

_____

_____

_____

_____

Clear You're Mind

This is Important.

Get anything out of your head that may be a distraction from today's goal on this page.

Day 20

What is today's main goal? Make sure this step will get you closer to your 100 day goal.

_____

Why do you want to achieve this goal? Be specific. Give this goal a meaning.

_____

_____

_____

_____

_____

_____

Write three ways you can accomplish today's main goal.

_____

_____

_____

_____

_____

_____

Clear You're Mind

This is Important.

Get anything out of your head that may be a distraction from today's goal on this page.

10 Day Review

Rate how you feel you did these past 10 days.

1 being poor, 10 being excellent

1 2 3 4 5 6 7 8 9 10

How close are you to your 100 day goal?

_____

_____

_____

Name the things you wish you could have accomplished, but did not these past 10 days.

_____

_____

_____

_____

3rd 10 Day Plan of Attack

What is your main goal you want to achieve in 100 days?

_____

Name three major steps you would like to achieve these next 10 days.

_____

_____

_____

Schedule your major steps for the next Ten Days.

Day One: _____

Day Two: _____

Day Three: _____

Day Four: _____

Day Five: _____

Day Six: _____

Day Seven: _____

Day Eight: _____

Day Nine: _____

Day Ten: _____

Day 21

What is today's main goal? Make sure this step will get you closer to your 100 day goal.

_____

Why do you want to achieve this goal? Be specific. Give this goal a meaning.

_____

_____

_____

_____

_____

_____

Write three ways you can accomplish today's main goal.

_____

_____

_____

_____

_____

_____

Clear You're Mind

This is Important.

Get anything out of your head that may be a distraction from today's goal on this page.

Day 22

What is today's main goal? Make sure this step will get you closer to your 100 day goal.

_____

Why do you want to achieve this goal? Be specific. Give this goal a meaning.

_____

_____

_____

_____

_____

Write three ways you can accomplish today's main goal.

_____

_____

_____

_____

_____

Clear You're Mind

This is Important.

Get anything out of your head that may be a distraction from today's goal on this page.

Day 23

What is today's main goal? Make sure this step will get you closer to your 100 day goal.

_____

Why do you want to achieve this goal? Be specific. Give this goal a meaning.

_____

_____

_____

_____

_____

_____

Write three ways you can accomplish today's main goal.

_____

_____

_____

_____

_____

_____

Clear You're Mind

This is Important.

Get anything out of your head that may be a distraction from today's goal on this page.

Day 24

What is today's main goal? Make sure this step will get you closer to your 100 day goal.

_____

Why do you want to achieve this goal? Be specific. Give this goal a meaning.

_____

_____

_____

_____

_____

_____

Write three ways you can accomplish today's main goal.

_____

_____

_____

_____

_____

_____

Clear You're Mind

This is Important.

Get anything out of your head that may be a distraction from today's goal on this page.

Day 25

What is today's main goal? Make sure this step will get you closer to your 100 day goal.

_____

Why do you want to achieve this goal? Be specific. Give this goal a meaning.

_____

_____

_____

_____

_____

_____

Write three ways you can accomplish today's main goal.

_____

_____

_____

_____

_____

_____

Clear You're Mind

This is Important.

Get anything out of your head that may be a distraction from today's goal on this page.

Day 26

What is today's main goal? Make sure this step will get you closer to your 100 day goal.

_____

Why do you want to achieve this goal? Be specific. Give this goal a meaning.

_____

_____

_____

_____

_____

_____

Write three ways you can accomplish today's main goal.

_____

_____

_____

_____

_____

Clear You're Mind

This is Important.

Get anything out of your head that may be a distraction from today's goal on this page.

Day 27

What is today's main goal? Make sure this step will get you closer to your 100 day goal.

_____

Why do you want to achieve this goal? Be specific. Give this goal a meaning.

_____

_____

_____

_____

_____

Write three ways you can accomplish today's main goal.

_____

_____

_____

_____

_____

Clear You're Mind

This is Important.

Get anything out of your head that may be a distraction from today's goal on this page.

Day 28

What is today's main goal? Make sure this step will get you closer to your 100 day goal.

_____

Why do you want to achieve this goal? Be specific. Give this goal a meaning.

_____

_____

_____

_____

_____

Write three ways you can accomplish today's main goal.

_____

_____

_____

_____

_____

_____

Clear You're Mind

This is Important.

Get anything out of your head that may be a distraction from today's goal on this page.

Day 29

What is today's main goal? Make sure this step will get you closer to your 100 day goal.

_____

Why do you want to achieve this goal? Be specific. Give this goal a meaning.

_____

_____

_____

_____

_____

Write three ways you can accomplish today's main goal.

_____

_____

_____

_____

_____

Clear You're Mind

This is Important.

Get anything out of your head that may be a distraction from today's goal on this page.

Day 30

What is today's main goal? Make sure this step will get you closer to your 100 day goal.

_____

Why do you want to achieve this goal? Be specific. Give this goal a meaning.

_____

_____

_____

_____

_____

Write three ways you can accomplish today's main goal.

_____

_____

_____

_____

_____

Clear You're Mind

This is Important.

Get anything out of your head that may be a distraction from today's goal on this page.

10 Day Review

Rate how you feel you did these past 10 days.

1 being poor, 10 being excellent

1 2 3 4 5 6 7 8 9 10

How close are you to your 100 day goal?

_____

_____

_____

Name the things you wish you could have accomplished, but did not these past 10 days.

_____

_____

_____

_____

4th 10 Day Plan of Attack

What is your main goal you want to achieve in 100 days?

_____

Name three major steps you would like to achieve these next 10 days.

_____

_____

_____

Schedule your major steps for the next Ten Days.

Day One: _____

Day Two: _____

Day Three: _____

Day Four: _____

Day Five: _____

Day Six: _____

Day Seven: _____

Day Eight: _____

Day Nine: _____

Day Ten: _____

Day 31

What is today's main goal? Make sure this step will get you closer to your 100 day goal.

_____

Why do you want to achieve this goal? Be specific. Give this goal a meaning.

_____

_____

_____

_____

_____

Write three ways you can accomplish today's main goal.

_____

_____

_____

_____

_____

Clear You're Mind

This is Important.

Get anything out of your head that may be a distraction from today's goal on this page.

.

Day 32

What is today's main goal? Make sure this step will get you closer to your 100 day goal.

_____

Why do you want to achieve this goal? Be specific. Give this goal a meaning.

_____

_____

_____

_____

_____

Write three ways you can accomplish today's main goal.

_____

_____

_____

_____

_____

Clear You're Mind

This is Important.

Get anything out of your head that may be a distraction from today's goal on this page.

Day 33

What is today's main goal? Make sure this step will get you closer to your 100 day goal.

_____

Why do you want to achieve this goal? Be specific. Give this goal a meaning.

_____

_____

_____

_____

_____

_____

Write three ways you can accomplish today's main goal.

_____

_____

_____

_____

_____

_____

Clear You're Mind

This is Important.

Get anything out of your head that may be a distraction from today's goal on this page.

Day 34

What is today's main goal? Make sure this step will get you closer to your 100 day goal.

_____

Why do you want to achieve this goal? Be specific. Give this goal a meaning.

_____

_____

_____

_____

_____

_____

Write three ways you can accomplish today's main goal.

_____

_____

_____

_____

_____

_____

Clear You're Mind

This is Important.

Get anything out of your head that may be a distraction from today's goal on this page.

Day 35

What is today's main goal? Make sure this step will get you closer to your 100 day goal.

_____

Why do you want to achieve this goal? Be specific. Give this goal a meaning.

_____

_____

_____

_____

_____

Write three ways you can accomplish today's main goal.

_____

_____

_____

_____

_____

Clear You're Mind

This is Important.

Get anything out of your head that may be a distraction from today's goal on this page.

Day 36

What is today's main goal? Make sure this step will get you closer to your 100 day goal.

_____

Why do you want to achieve this goal? Be specific. Give this goal a meaning.

_____

_____

_____

_____

_____

_____

Write three ways you can accomplish today's main goal.

_____

_____

_____

_____

_____

_____

Clear You're Mind

This is Important.

Get anything out of your head that may be a distraction from today's goal on this page.

REMINDER- THIS JOURNAL DOESN'T WORK IF YOU DON'T.

Day 37

What is today's main goal? Make sure this step will get you closer to your 100 day goal.

_____

Why do you want to achieve this goal? Be specific. Give this goal a meaning.

_____

_____

_____

_____

_____

_____

Write three ways you can accomplish today's main goal.

_____

_____

_____

_____

_____

_____

Clear You're Mind

This is Important.

Get anything out of your head that may be a distraction from today's goal on this page.

Day 38

What is today's main goal? Make sure this step will get you closer to your 100 day goal.

_____

Why do you want to achieve this goal? Be specific. Give this goal a meaning.

_____

_____

_____

_____

_____

Write three ways you can accomplish today's main goal.

_____

_____

_____

_____

_____

Clear You're Mind

This is Important.

Get anything out of your head that may be a distraction from today's goal on this page.

Day 39

What is today's main goal? Make sure this step will get you closer to your 100 day goal.

_____

Why do you want to achieve this goal? Be specific. Give this goal a meaning.

_____

_____

_____

_____

_____

_____

Write three ways you can accomplish today's main goal.

_____

_____

_____

_____

_____

_____

Clear You're Mind

This is Important.

Get anything out of your head that may be a distraction from today's goal on this page.

Day 40

What is today's main goal? Make sure this step will get you closer to your 100 day goal.

_____

Why do you want to achieve this goal? Be specific. Give this goal a meaning.

_____

_____

_____

_____

_____

_____

Write three ways you can accomplish today's main goal.

_____

_____

_____

_____

_____

_____

Clear You're Mind

This is Important.

Get anything out of your head that may be a distraction from today's goal on this page.

10 Day Review

Rate how you feel you did these past 10 days.

1 being poor, 10 being excellent

1 2 3 4 5 6 7 8 9 10

How close are you to your 100 day goal?

_____

_____

_____

Name the things you wish you could have accomplished, but did not these past 10 days.

_____

_____

_____

_____

5th 10 Day Plan of Attack

What is your main goal you want to achieve in 100 days?

_____

Name three major steps you would like to achieve these next 10 days.

_____

_____

_____

Schedule your major steps for the next Ten Days.

Day One: _____

Day Two: _____

Day Three: _____

Day Four: _____

Day Five: _____

Day Six: _____

Day Seven: _____

Day Eight: _____

Day Nine: _____

Day Ten: _____

Day 41

What is today's main goal? Make sure this step will get you closer to your 100 day goal.

_____

Why do you want to achieve this goal? Be specific. Give this goal a meaning.

_____

_____

_____

_____

_____

_____

Write three ways you can accomplish today's main goal.

_____

_____

_____

_____

_____

_____

Clear You're Mind

This is Important.

Get anything out of your head that may be a distraction from today's goal on this page.

'

Day 42

What is today's main goal? Make sure this step will get you closer to your 100 day goal.

_____

Why do you want to achieve this goal? Be specific. Give this goal a meaning.

_____

_____

_____

_____

_____

_____

Write three ways you can accomplish today's main goal.

_____

_____

_____

_____

_____

_____

Clear You're Mind

This is Important.

Get anything out of your head that may be a distraction from today's goal on this page.

Day 43

What is today's main goal? Make sure this step will get you closer to your 100 day goal.

_____

Why do you want to achieve this goal? Be specific. Give this goal a meaning.

_____

_____

_____

_____

_____

Write three ways you can accomplish today's main goal.

_____

_____

_____

_____

_____

Clear You're Mind

This is Important.

Get anything out of your head that may be a distraction from today's goal on this page.

Day 44

What is today's main goal? Make sure this step will get you closer to your 100 day goal.

_____

Why do you want to achieve this goal? Be specific. Give this goal a meaning.

_____

_____

_____

_____

_____

_____

Write three ways you can accomplish today's main goal.

_____

_____

_____

_____

_____

_____

Clear You're Mind

This is Important.

Get anything out of your head that may be a distraction from today's goal on this page.

Day 45

What is today's main goal? Make sure this step will get you closer to your 100 day goal.

_____

Why do you want to achieve this goal? Be specific. Give this goal a meaning.

_____

_____

_____

_____

_____

_____

Write three ways you can accomplish today's main goal.

_____

_____

_____

_____

_____

_____

Clear You're Mind

This is Important.

Get anything out of your head that may be a distraction from today's goal on this page.

Day 46

What is today's main goal? Make sure this step will get you closer to your 100 day goal.

_____

Why do you want to achieve this goal? Be specific. Give this goal a meaning.

_____

_____

_____

_____

_____

_____

Write three ways you can accomplish today's main goal.

_____

_____

_____

_____

_____

_____

Clear You're Mind

This is Important.

Get anything out of your head that may be a distraction from today's goal on this page.

Day 47

What is today's main goal? Make sure this step will get you closer to your 100 day goal.

_____

Why do you want to achieve this goal? Be specific. Give this goal a meaning.

_____

_____

_____

_____

_____

Write three ways you can accomplish today's main goal.

_____

_____

_____

_____

_____

Clear You're Mind

This is Important.

Get anything out of your head that may be a distraction from today's goal on this page.

Day 48

What is today's main goal? Make sure this step will get you closer to your 100 day goal.

_____

Why do you want to achieve this goal? Be specific. Give this goal a meaning.

_____

_____

_____

_____

_____

Write three ways you can accomplish today's main goal.

_____

_____

_____

_____

_____

Clear You're Mind

This is Important.

Get anything out of your head that may be a distraction from today's goal on this page.

Day 49

What is today's main goal? Make sure this step will get you closer to your 100 day goal.

_____

Why do you want to achieve this goal? Be specific. Give this goal a meaning.

_____

_____

_____

_____

_____

_____

Write three ways you can accomplish today's main goal.

_____

_____

_____

_____

_____

_____

Clear You're Mind

This is Important.

Get anything out of your head that may be a distraction from today's goal on this page.

Day 50

What is today's main goal? Make sure this step will get you closer to your 100 day goal.

_____

Why do you want to achieve this goal? Be specific. Give this goal a meaning.

_____

_____

_____

_____

_____

_____

Write three ways you can accomplish today's main goal.

_____

_____

_____

_____

_____

_____

Clear You're Mind

This is Important.

Get anything out of your head that may be a distraction from today's goal on this page.

10 Day Review

Rate how you feel you did these past 10 days.

1 being poor, 10 being excellent

1 2 3 4 5 6 7 8 9 10

How close are you to your 100 day goal?

_____

_____

_____

Name the things you wish you could have accomplished, but did not these past 10 days.

_____

_____

_____

_____

6th 10 Day Plan of Attack

What is your main goal you want to achieve in 100 days?

_____

Name three major steps you would like to achieve these next 10 days.

_____

_____

_____

Schedule your major steps for the next Ten Days.

Day One: _____

Day Two: _____

Day Three: _____

Day Four: _____

Day Five: _____

Day Six: _____

Day Seven: _____

Day Eight: _____

Day Nine: _____

Day Ten: _____

Day 51

What is today's main goal? Make sure this step will get you closer to your 100 day goal.

_____

Why do you want to achieve this goal? Be specific. Give this goal a meaning.

_____

_____

_____

_____

_____

_____

Write three ways you can accomplish today's main goal.

_____

_____

_____

_____

_____

_____

Clear You're Mind

This is Important.

Get anything out of your head that may be a distraction from today's goal on this page.

Day 52

What is today's main goal? Make sure this step will get you closer to your 100 day goal.

_____

Why do you want to achieve this goal? Be specific. Give this goal a meaning.

_____

_____

_____

_____

_____

Write three ways you can accomplish today's main goal.

_____

_____

_____

_____

_____

_____

Clear You're Mind

This is Important.

Get anything out of your head that may be a distraction from today's goal on this page.

Day 53

What is today's main goal? Make sure this step will get you closer to your 100 day goal.

_____

Why do you want to achieve this goal? Be specific. Give this goal a meaning.

_____

_____

_____

_____

_____

Write three ways you can accomplish today's main goal.

_____

_____

_____

_____

_____

_____

Clear You're Mind

This is Important.

Get anything out of your head that may be a distraction from today's goal on this page.

Day 54

What is today's main goal? Make sure this step will get you closer to your 100 day goal.

_____

Why do you want to achieve this goal? Be specific. Give this goal a meaning.

_____

_____

_____

_____

_____

Write three ways you can accomplish today's main goal.

_____

_____

_____

_____

_____

Clear You're Mind

This is Important.

Get anything out of your head that may be a distraction from today's goal on this page.

Day 55

What is today's main goal? Make sure this step will get you closer to your 100 day goal.

_____

Why do you want to achieve this goal? Be specific. Give this goal a meaning.

_____

_____

_____

_____

_____

Write three ways you can accomplish today's main goal.

_____

_____

_____

_____

_____

Clear You're Mind

This is Important.

Get anything out of your head that may be a distraction from today's goal on this page.

REMINDER- THIS JOURNAL DOESN'T WORK IF YOU DON'T.

Day 56

What is today's main goal? Make sure this step will get you closer to your 100 day goal.

_____

Why do you want to achieve this goal? Be specific. Give this goal a meaning.

_____

_____

_____

_____

_____

_____

Write three ways you can accomplish today's main goal.

_____

_____

_____

_____

_____

_____

Clear You're Mind

This is Important.

Get anything out of your head that may be a distraction from today's goal on this page.

Day 57

What is today's main goal? Make sure this step will get you closer to your 100 day goal.

_____

Why do you want to achieve this goal? Be specific. Give this goal a meaning.

_____

_____

_____

_____

_____

_____

Write three ways you can accomplish today's main goal.

_____

_____

_____

_____

_____

_____

Clear You're Mind

This is Important.

Get anything out of your head that may be a distraction from today's goal on this page.

Day 58

What is today's main goal? Make sure this step will get you closer to your 100 day goal.

_____

Why do you want to achieve this goal? Be specific. Give this goal a meaning.

_____

_____

_____

_____

_____

_____

Write three ways you can accomplish today's main goal.

_____

_____

_____

_____

_____

_____

Clear You're Mind

This is Important.

Get anything out of your head that may be a distraction from today's goal on this page.

Day 59

What is today's main goal? Make sure this step will get you closer to your 100 day goal.

_____

Why do you want to achieve this goal? Be specific. Give this goal a meaning.

_____

_____

_____

_____

_____

Write three ways you can accomplish today's main goal.

_____

_____

_____

_____

_____

Clear You're Mind

This is Important.

Get anything out of your head that may be a distraction from today's goal on this page.

Day 60

What is today's main goal? Make sure this step will get you closer to your 100 day goal.

_____

Why do you want to achieve this goal? Be specific. Give this goal a meaning.

_____

_____

_____

_____

_____

Write three ways you can accomplish today's main goal.

_____

_____

_____

_____

_____

_____

Clear You're Mind

This is Important.

Get anything out of your head that may be a distraction from today's goal on this page.

10 Day Review

Rate how you feel you did these past 10 days.

1 being poor, 10 being excellent

1 2 3 4 5 6 7 8 9 10

How close are you to your 100 day goal?

_____

_____

_____

Name the things you wish you could have accomplished, but did not these past 10 days.

_____

_____

_____

_____

7th 10 Day Plan of Attack

What is your main goal you want to achieve in 100 days?

_____

Name three major steps you would like to achieve these next 10 days.

_____

_____

_____

Schedule your major steps for the next Ten Days.

Day One: _____

Day Two: _____

Day Three: _____

Day Four: _____

Day Five: _____

Day Six: _____

Day Seven: _____

Day Eight: _____

Day Nine: _____

Day Ten: _____

Day 61

What is today's main goal? Make sure this step will get you closer to your 100 day goal.

_____

Why do you want to achieve this goal? Be specific. Give this goal a meaning.

_____

_____

_____

_____

_____

Write three ways you can accomplish today's main goal.

_____

_____

_____

_____

_____

_____

Clear You're Mind

This is Important.

Get anything out of your head that may be a distraction from today's goal on this page.

Day 62

What is today's main goal? Make sure this step will get you closer to your 100 day goal.

_____

Why do you want to achieve this goal? Be specific. Give this goal a meaning.

_____

_____

_____

_____

_____

Write three ways you can accomplish today's main goal.

_____

_____

_____

_____

_____

Clear You're Mind

This is Important.

Get anything out of your head that may be a distraction from today's goal on this page.

Day 63

What is today's main goal? Make sure this step will get you closer to your 100 day goal.

_____

Why do you want to achieve this goal? Be specific. Give this goal a meaning.

_____

_____

_____

_____

_____

Write three ways you can accomplish today's main goal.

_____

_____

_____

_____

_____

_____

Clear You're Mind

This is Important.

Get anything out of your head that may be a distraction from today's goal on this page.

Day 64

What is today's main goal? Make sure this step will get you closer to your 100 day goal.

_____

Why do you want to achieve this goal? Be specific. Give this goal a meaning.

_____

_____

_____

_____

_____

Write three ways you can accomplish today's main goal.

_____

_____

_____

_____

_____

Clear You're Mind

This is Important.

Get anything out of your head that may be a distraction from today's goal on this page.

Day 65

What is today's main goal? Make sure this step will get you closer to your 100 day goal.

_____

Why do you want to achieve this goal? Be specific. Give this goal a meaning.

_____

_____

_____

_____

_____

Write three ways you can accomplish today's main goal.

_____

_____

_____

_____

_____

Clear You're Mind

This is Important.

Get anything out of your head that may be a distraction from today's goal on this page.

Day 66

What is today's main goal? Make sure this step will get you closer to your 100 day goal.

_____

Why do you want to achieve this goal? Be specific. Give this goal a meaning.

_____

_____

_____

_____

_____

Write three ways you can accomplish today's main goal.

_____

_____

_____

_____

_____

_____

Clear You're Mind

This is Important.

Get anything out of your head that may be a distraction from today's goal on this page.

Day 67

What is today's main goal? Make sure this step will get you closer to your 100 day goal.

_____

Why do you want to achieve this goal? Be specific. Give this goal a meaning.

_____

_____

_____

_____

_____

_____

Write three ways you can accomplish today's main goal.

_____

_____

_____

_____

_____

_____

Clear You're Mind

This is Important.

Get anything out of your head that may be a distraction from today's goal on this page.

REMINDER- THIS JOURNAL DOESN'T WORK IF YOU DON'T.

Day 68

What is today's main goal? Make sure this step will get you closer to your 100 day goal.

_____

Why do you want to achieve this goal? Be specific. Give this goal a meaning.

_____

_____

_____

_____

_____

Write three ways you can accomplish today's main goal.

_____

_____

_____

_____

_____

Clear You're Mind

This is Important.

Get anything out of your head that may be a distraction from today's goal on this page.

Day 69

What is today's main goal? Make sure this step will get you closer to your 100 day goal.

_____

Why do you want to achieve this goal? Be specific. Give this goal a meaning.

_____

_____

_____

_____

_____

Write three ways you can accomplish today's main goal.

_____

_____

_____

_____

_____

_____

Clear You're Mind

This is Important.

Get anything out of your head that may be a distraction from today's goal on this page.

Day 70

What is today's main goal? Make sure this step will get you closer to your 100 day goal.

_____

Why do you want to achieve this goal? Be specific. Give this goal a meaning.

_____

_____

_____

_____

_____

_____

Write three ways you can accomplish today's main goal.

_____

_____

_____

_____

_____

_____

Clear You're Mind

This is Important.

Get anything out of your head that may be a distraction from today's goal on this page.

10 Day Review

Rate how you feel you did these past 10 days.

1 being poor, 10 being excellent

1 2 3 4 5 6 7 8 9 10

How close are you to your 100 day goal?

_____

_____

_____

Name the things you wish you could have accomplished, but did not these past 10 days.

_____

_____

_____

_____

8th 10 Day Plan of Attack

What is your main goal you want to achieve in 100 days?

_____

Name three major steps you would like to achieve these next 10 days.

_____

_____

_____

Schedule your major steps for the next Ten Days.

Day One: _____

Day Two: _____

Day Three: _____

Day Four: _____

Day Five: _____

Day Six: _____

Day Seven: _____

Day Eight: _____

Day Nine: _____

Day Ten: _____

Day 71

What is today's main goal? Make sure this step will get you closer to your 100 day goal.

_____

Why do you want to achieve this goal? Be specific. Give this goal a meaning.

_____

_____

_____

_____

_____

Write three ways you can accomplish today's main goal.

_____

_____

_____

_____

_____

Clear You're Mind

. This is Important.

Get anything out of your head that may be a distraction from today's goal on this page.

REMINDER- THIS JOURNAL DOESN'T WORK IF YOU DON'T.

Day 72

What is today's main goal? Make sure this step will get you closer to your 100 day goal.

_____

Why do you want to achieve this goal? Be specific. Give this goal a meaning.

_____

_____

_____

_____

_____

Write three ways you can accomplish today's main goal.

_____

_____

_____

_____

_____

_____

Clear You're Mind

This is Important.

Get anything out of your head that may be a distraction from today's goal on this page.

Day 73

What is today's main goal? Make sure this step will get you closer to your 100 day goal.

_____

Why do you want to achieve this goal? Be specific. Give this goal a meaning.

_____

_____

_____

_____

_____

_____

Write three ways you can accomplish today's main goal.

_____

_____

_____

_____

_____

_____

Clear You're Mind

This is Important.

Get anything out of your head that may be a distraction from today's goal on this page.

Day 74

What is today's main goal? Make sure this step will get you closer to your 100 day goal.

_____

Why do you want to achieve this goal? Be specific. Give this goal a meaning.

_____

_____

_____

_____

_____

Write three ways you can accomplish today's main goal.

_____

_____

_____

_____

_____

_____

Clear You're Mind

This is Important.

Get anything out of your head that may be a distraction from today's goal on this page.

REMINDER- THIS JOURNAL DOESN'T WORK IF YOU DON'T.

Day 75

What is today's main goal? Make sure this step will get you closer to your 100 day goal.

_____

Why do you want to achieve this goal? Be specific. Give this goal a meaning.

_____

_____

_____

_____

_____

Write three ways you can accomplish today's main goal.

_____

_____

_____

_____

_____

Clear You're Mind

This is Important.

Get anything out of your head that may be a distraction from today's goal on this page.

Day 76

What is today's main goal? Make sure this step will get you closer to your 100 day goal.

_____

Why do you want to achieve this goal? Be specific. Give this goal a meaning.

_____

_____

_____

_____

_____

Write three ways you can accomplish today's main goal.

_____

_____

_____

_____

_____

_____

Clear You're Mind

This is Important.

Get anything out of your head that may be a distraction from today's goal on this page.

Day 77

What is today's main goal? Make sure this step will get you closer to your 100 day goal.

_____

Why do you want to achieve this goal? Be specific. Give this goal a meaning.

_____

_____

_____

_____

_____

Write three ways you can accomplish today's main goal.

_____

_____

_____

_____

_____

Clear You're Mind

This is Important.

Get anything out of your head that may be a distraction from today's goal on this page.

Day 78

What is today's main goal? Make sure this step will get you closer to your 100 day goal.

_____

Why do you want to achieve this goal? Be specific. Give this goal a meaning.

_____

_____

_____

_____

_____

Write three ways you can accomplish today's main goal.

_____

_____

_____

_____

_____

_____

Clear You're Mind

This is Important.

Get anything out of your head that may be a distraction from today's goal on this page.

Day 79

What is today's main goal? Make sure this step will get you closer to your 100 day goal.

_____

Why do you want to achieve this goal? Be specific. Give this goal a meaning.

_____

_____

_____

_____

_____

Write three ways you can accomplish today's main goal.

_____

_____

_____

_____

_____

_____

Clear You're Mind

This is Important.

Get anything out of your head that may be a distraction from today's goal on this page.

Day 80

What is today's main goal? Make sure this step will get you closer to your 100 day goal.

_____

Why do you want to achieve this goal? Be specific. Give this goal a meaning.

_____

_____

_____

_____

_____

_____

Write three ways you can accomplish today's main goal.

_____

_____

_____

_____

_____

_____

Clear You're Mind

This is Important.

Get anything out of your head that may be a distraction from today's goal on this page.

10 Day Review

Rate how you feel you did these past 10 days.

1 being poor, 10 being excellent

1 2 3 4 5 6 7 8 9 10

How close are you to your 100 day goal?

_____

_____

_____

Name the things you wish you could have accomplished, but did not these past 10 days.

_____

_____

_____

_____

9th 10 Day Plan of Attack

What is your main goal you want to achieve in 100 days?

_____

Name three major steps you would like to achieve these next 10 days.

_____

_____

_____

Schedule your major steps for the next Ten Days.

Day One: _____

Day Two: _____

Day Three: _____

Day Four: _____

Day Five: _____

Day Six: _____

Day Seven: _____

Day Eight: _____

Day Nine: _____

Day Ten: _____

Day 81

What is today's main goal? Make sure this step will get you closer to your 100 day goal.

_____

Why do you want to achieve this goal? Be specific. Give this goal a meaning.

_____

_____

_____

_____

_____

_____

Write three ways you can accomplish today's main goal.

_____

_____

_____

_____

_____

_____

Clear You're Mind

This is Important.

Get anything out of your head that may be a distraction from today's goal on this page.

Day 82

What is today's main goal? Make sure this step will get you closer to your 100 day goal.

_____

Why do you want to achieve this goal? Be specific. Give this goal a meaning.

_____

_____

_____

_____

_____

Write three ways you can accomplish today's main goal.

_____

_____

_____

_____

_____

Clear You're Mind

This is Important.

Get anything out of your head that may be a distraction from today's goal on this page.

Day 83

What is today's main goal? Make sure this step will get you closer to your 100 day goal.

_____

Why do you want to achieve this goal? Be specific. Give this goal a meaning.

_____

_____

_____

_____

_____

Write three ways you can accomplish today's main goal.

_____

_____

_____

_____

_____

Clear You're Mind

This is Important.

Get anything out of your head that may be a distraction from today's goal on this page.

Day 84

What is today's main goal? Make sure this step will get you closer to your 100 day goal.

_____

Why do you want to achieve this goal? Be specific. Give this goal a meaning.

_____

_____

_____

_____

_____

Write three ways you can accomplish today's main goal.

_____

_____

_____

_____

_____

_____

Clear You're Mind

This is Important.

Get anything out of your head that may be a distraction from today's goal on this page.

Day 85

What is today's main goal? Make sure this step will get you closer to your 100 day goal.

_____

Why do you want to achieve this goal? Be specific. Give this goal a meaning.

_____

_____

_____

_____

_____

_____

Write three ways you can accomplish today's main goal.

_____

_____

_____

_____

_____

_____

Clear You're Mind

This is Important.

Get anything out of your head that may be a distraction from today's goal on this page.

REMINDER- THIS JOURNAL DOESN'T WORK IF YOU DON'T.

Day 86

What is today's main goal? Make sure this step will get you closer to your 100 day goal.

_____

Why do you want to achieve this goal? Be specific. Give this goal a meaning.

_____

_____

_____

_____

_____

_____

Write three ways you can accomplish today's main goal.

_____

_____

_____

_____

_____

_____

Clear You're Mind

This is Important.

Get anything out of your head that may be a distraction from today's goal on this page.

Day 87

What is today's main goal? Make sure this step will get you closer to your 100 day goal.

_____

Why do you want to achieve this goal? Be specific. Give this goal a meaning.

_____

_____

_____

_____

_____

Write three ways you can accomplish today's main goal.

_____

_____

_____

_____

_____

_____

Clear You're Mind

This is Important.

Get anything out of your head that may be a distraction from today's goal on this page.

Day 88

What is today's main goal? Make sure this step will get you closer to your 100 day goal.

_____

Why do you want to achieve this goal? Be specific. Give this goal a meaning.

_____

_____

_____

_____

_____

Write three ways you can accomplish today's main goal.

_____

_____

_____

_____

_____

_____

Clear You're Mind

This is Important.

Get anything out of your head that may be a distraction from today's goal on this page.

REMINDER- THIS JOURNAL DOESN'T WORK IF YOU DON'T.

Day 89

What is today's main goal? Make sure this step will get you closer to your 100 day goal.

_____

Why do you want to achieve this goal? Be specific. Give this goal a meaning.

_____

_____

_____

_____

_____

_____

Write three ways you can accomplish today's main goal.

_____

_____

_____

_____

_____

_____

Clear You're Mind

This is Important.

Get anything out of your head that may be a distraction from today's goal on this page.

REMINDER- THIS JOURNAL DOESN'T WORK IF YOU DON'T.

Day 90

What is today's main goal? Make sure this step will get you closer to your 100 day goal.

_____

Why do you want to achieve this goal? Be specific. Give this goal a meaning.

_____

_____

_____

_____

_____

_____

Write three ways you can accomplish today's main goal.

_____

_____

_____

_____

_____

_____

Clear You're Mind

This is Important.

Get anything out of your head that may be a distraction from today's goal on this page.

REMINDER- THIS JOURNAL DOESN'T WORK IF YOU DON'T.

10 Day Review

Rate how you feel you did these past 10 days.

1 being poor, 10 being excellent

1 2 3 4 5 6 7 8 9 10

How close are you to your 100 day goal?

_____

_____

_____

Name the things you wish you could have accomplished, but did not these past 10 days.

_____

_____

_____

_____

10th 10 Day Plan of Attack

What is your main goal you want to achieve in 100 days?

_____

Name three major steps you would like to achieve these next 10 days.

_____

_____

_____

Schedule your major steps for the next Ten Days.

Day One: _____

Day Two: _____

Day Three: _____

Day Four: _____

Day Five: _____

Day Six: _____

Day Seven: _____

Day Eight: _____

Day Nine: _____

Day Ten: _____

Day 91

What is today's main goal? Make sure this step will get you closer to your 100 day goal.

_____

Why do you want to achieve this goal? Be specific. Give this goal a meaning.

_____

_____

_____

_____

_____

_____

Write three ways you can accomplish today's main goal.

_____

_____

_____

_____

_____

_____

Clear You're Mind

This is Important.

Get anything out of your head that may be a distraction from today's goal on this page.

Day 92

What is today's main goal? Make sure this step will get you closer to your 100 day goal.

_____

Why do you want to achieve this goal? Be specific. Give this goal a meaning.

_____

_____

_____

_____

_____

_____

Write three ways you can accomplish today's main goal.

_____

_____

_____

_____

_____

_____

Clear You're Mind

This is Important.

Get anything out of your head that may be a distraction from today's goal on this page.

REMINDER- THIS JOURNAL DOESN'T WORK IF YOU DON'T.

Day 93

What is today's main goal? Make sure this step will get you closer to your 100 day goal.

_____

Why do you want to achieve this goal? Be specific. Give this goal a meaning.

_____

_____

_____

_____

_____

Write three ways you can accomplish today's main goal.

_____

_____

_____

_____

_____

_____

Clear You're Mind

This is Important.

Get anything out of your head that may be a distraction from today's goal on this page.

Day 94

What is today's main goal? Make sure this step will get you closer to your 100 day goal.

_____

Why do you want to achieve this goal? Be specific. Give this goal a meaning.

_____

_____

_____

_____

_____

Write three ways you can accomplish today's main goal.

_____

_____

_____

_____

_____

_____

Clear You're Mind

This is Important.

Get anything out of your head that may be a distraction from today's goal on this page.

Day 95

What is today's main goal? Make sure this step will get you closer to your 100 day goal.

_____

Why do you want to achieve this goal? Be specific. Give this goal a meaning.

_____

_____

_____

_____

_____

Write three ways you can accomplish today's main goal.

_____

_____

_____

_____

_____

_____

Clear You're Mind

This is Important.

Get anything out of your head that may be a distraction from today's goal on this page.

Day 96

What is today's main goal? Make sure this step will get you closer to your 100 day goal.

_____

Why do you want to achieve this goal? Be specific. Give this goal a meaning.

_____

_____

_____

_____

_____

_____

Write three ways you can accomplish today's main goal.

_____

_____

_____

_____

_____

_____

Clear You're Mind

This is Important.

Get anything out of your head that may be a distraction from today's goal on this page.

Day 97

What is today's main goal? Make sure this step will get you closer to your 100 day goal.

_____

Why do you want to achieve this goal? Be specific. Give this goal a meaning.

_____

_____

_____

_____

_____

Write three ways you can accomplish today's main goal.

_____

_____

_____

_____

_____

_____

Clear You're Mind

This is Important.

Get anything out of your head that may be a distraction from today's goal on this page.

REMINDER- THIS JOURNAL DOESN'T WORK IF YOU DON'T.

Day 98

What is today's main goal? Make sure this step will get you closer to your 100 day goal.

_____

Why do you want to achieve this goal? Be specific. Give this goal a meaning.

_____

_____

_____

_____

_____

Write three ways you can accomplish today's main goal.

_____

_____

_____

_____

_____

Clear You're Mind

This is Important.

Get anything out of your head that may be a distraction from today's goal on this page.

Day 99

What is today's main goal? Make sure this step will get you closer to your 100 day goal.

_____

Why do you want to achieve this goal? Be specific. Give this goal a meaning.

_____

_____

_____

_____

_____

_____

Write three ways you can accomplish today's main goal.

_____

_____

_____

_____

_____

_____

Clear You're Mind

This is Important.

Get anything out of your head that may be a distraction from today's goal on this page.

Day 100

What is today's main goal? Make sure this step will get you closer to your 100 day goal.

_____

Why do you want to achieve this goal? Be specific. Give this goal a meaning.

_____

_____

_____

_____

_____

_____

Write three ways you can accomplish today's main goal.

_____

_____

_____

_____

_____

_____

Clear You're Mind

This is Important.

Get anything out of your head that may be a distraction from today's goal on this page.

100 Day Review

Rate how you feel you did these past 100 days.

1 being poor, 10 being excellent

1 2 3 4 5 6 7 8 9 10

Did you achieve your 100 day goal?

_____

_____

Are you satisfied with your success?

_____

_____

_____

Write a few important things you have learned that will make your next 100 days go by smoother and achieve your goals faster.

_____

_____

_____

_____

_____

_____

_____

Thank You For Using The-

Rise & Grind
Morning Success Journal

Love it or Hate it?

Please leave an honest

Review on Amazon.

#riseandgrindjournal

Tag Me On Instagram!

Personal Instagram / @JeremyWarlen

Business Instagram / @RetireBeforeYourParents

Made in the USA
Lexington, KY
22 March 2017